STAND YOUR GROUND

(The Biblical Foundation for Self-Defense)

Steve Jones

CONTENTS

INTRODUCTION

The fatal shooting of Trayvon Martin by George Zimmerman took place on the night of February 26, 2012, in Sanford, Florida. Six weeks later, amid widespread, intense and contradictory media coverage, a special prosecutor appointed by Governor Rick Scott charged Zimmerman with murder. Zimmerman's trial began on June 10, 2013, in Sanford. On July 13, 2013, a jury acquitted him of second-degree murder and of manslaughter charges.

Much controversy has followed that verdict, most of it centering upon the "Stand Your Ground" law in Florida and it's purported implications regarding race relations and the 2nd amendment to the U.S. Constitution. However, less frequently considered are the theological implications of the "Stand Your Ground" law in particular, and the right to self-defense in general.

There is a story of a Quaker who became exasperated with his cow. The cow swatted him in the face with her tail and he tried to restrain his anger. She kicked over the milk bucket and he tried to hold his temper. And then the cow kicked him in the shins and that was all he could take. Grabbing the cow by the horns he looked her square in the face and said "Thou knowest that I am a Quaker and I am a pacifist and I cannot hurt thee, but what thou doth not know is that tomorrow I'm going to sell thee to a Baptist."

As this little story illustrates, there are church denominations that teach their members to eschew all violence, even for the purpose of self-defense. Other church denominations do not. Why the difference? What does the Bible say? Is a Christian allowed to defend himself when attacked or does Jesus expect him to take a beating? Should a Christian procure a firearm to protect her home? Should a Christian acquire a concealed carry permit and "pack heat" everywhere he goes? Should a Christian lobby for more stringent gun control or should she join the National Rifle Association?

Most Christians have probably never heard a sermon on the subject of self-defense in general or the use of deadly force in self-defense in particular. However, the Bible is not silent on this subject. The issue is as timely now as it has ever been. The debate regarding the legitimate and illegitimate uses of force, particularly lethal force in self-defense, has certainly been in the forefront of the news lately. But even before the Martin shooting made headlines, thoughtful Christians struggled to harmonize Jesus' teaching to "turn the other cheek" with seemingly more aggressive Bible passages, not to mention the realities of life in an oftentimes violent world.

The current position of most Christians regarding personal self-defense seems to fall into one of the following three broadly representative categories.

1) Pacifism

Many Christian pacifists believe that it is wrong for a Christian to exercise force under any circumstances. A Christian pacifist typically would not serve in the military or law enforcement and would not use force to defend himself or others. As Philip Berrigan writes, "*We Christians forget (if we ever learned) that attempts to address real or imagined injustice by violent means are merely another exercise in denial - denial of God and her nonviolence towards us, denial of love of neighbor, denial of laws essential to our being."[1]*

2) Semi-Pacifism (my term)

This view allows that governments and their agents are authorized to use force but private citizens are not. Semi-pacifism is the assumed view of many if not most adherents to the "Just War" theory. The reason being that most versions of "Just War" theory delineate several limitations that must be present for the use of force in war to be considered just. One of those limitations invariably restricts the legitimate exercise of force to authorized government agents. Private citizens are not allowed to declare and wage war. Fair enough. However, this limitation to the use of force in war sometimes slips the bounds of that context and is applied to all uses of force. Thomas Aquinas wrote, *"It is not lawful for a man to intend killing a man in self-defense, except for such as have public authority, who while intending to kill a man in self-defense, refer this to the public good, as in the case of a soldier fighting against the foe, and in the minister of the judge struggling with robbers, although even these sin if they be moved by private animosity."[2]* Augustine wrote, *"I do not agree with the opinion that one may kill a man lest one be killed by him; unless one be a soldier, exercise a public office, so that one does it not for oneself, but for others, having the power to do so, provided it be in keeping with one's person."[3]*

More recently Arthur Holmes wrote, *"The use of force is limited to the state and its legally authorized agents; it is never the prerogative of individuals or parties within the state to use force on their own authority."[4]* Therefore, many Christians who

[1] Philip Berrigan, Fighting the Lamb's War: Skirmishes with the American Empire (iUniverse.com, 1996), 204.
[2] The Summa Theologica of St. Thomas Aquinas, Second and Revised Edition, 1920, www.newadvent.org/summa/3064.htm, (March 26, 2014).
[3] Nicene and Post-Nicene Fathers, First Series, Vol. 1. Edited by Philip Schaff. (Buffalo, NY: Christian Literature Publishing Co., 1887.) http://www.newadvent.org/fathers/1102047.htm. (March 26, 2014).
[4] Arthur F. Holmes, War and Christian Ethics (Baker, 1975), 5.

subscribe to the "Just War" theory might assume what I call a "semi-pacifist" stand as a part of the overall package. They believe that a Christian is permitted to serve in the military and/or law enforcement and may use force in the context of those professions, but only in that context. When the Christian takes off his uniform he forfeits the right to use force, as he is no longer an agent of the state. The theological reasoning given for this limitation is that God has established government for the purpose of justice and vengeance in society. Jack Cottrell writes, *"God himself has ordained government and appointed it as his own instrument for dispensing his own wrath and vengeance upon evildoers. God's stated will for governments is no less good and moral and righteous than his stated will for individuals. When government is carrying out its divinely specified functions, it is doing what is holy and righteous, especially when it is dispensing God's retributive justice upon evildoers."*[5] This is certainly true as far as it goes; however, in the minds of too many this truth is followed with an unfortunate non sequitur, i.e. that any individual/personal use of force is therefore forbidden because, by definition, it would constitute either retribution or vengeance on the part of the individual (functions rightfully restricted to the state). This assumption fails to recognize that the individual/personal use of force in self-defense might constitute a category other than vengeance or retribution, but more on that later.

3) Intuitive Guardianship

I created this third category to identify the legions of Christians (especially men) who have been taught only the first two positions on the use of force but who intuitively sense that neither position is appropriate when it comes to personal self-defense. They may not be able to articulate a

---

[5] Jack Cottrell, "JUST WAR? - A Valid Concept," *Christian Standard*, November 5, 2006.

Biblical apologetic for their desire to protect themselves, their families and loved ones but they sense it is the right thing to do. They know in their hearts that God has made them stewards, not only of their money, but also of their very lives and the lives of their families. They are faithful in that stewardship role, even if it requires the justifiable use of force and results in a scolding from believers of more fine tuned souls.

The purpose of this book is to move the third position beyond intuition and on to Biblically justifiable grounds. I believe that when we understand and obey what the Bible teaches on this subject of personal self-defense our lives will be improved in a number of ways. First, Christians will continue to practice self-defense but with a clear conscience due to its Biblical justification. Secondly, Christians will be even more eager to adopt the attitude and practice of self-restraint that is most likely to result in the prevention of violent conflict. And thirdly, it could save your life.

PART ONE

AN OLD TESTAMENT THEOLOGY
OF SELF-DEFENSE

Let us begin by looking at four Old Testament scriptures that help to establish the Biblical foundation for self-defense.

1) <u>**Exodus 20:13**</u> **"You shall not murder."**[6]

This commandment has been the source of much confusion and misapplication ever since the King James Version mistranslation, "Thou shalt not kill." Opponents of the justifiable use of lethal force appeal to this scripture as a prohibition from God against all killing under any circumstances. However, the sixth commandment should never be translated "Thou shall not kill," but rather, "You shall not murder." The Hebrew verb is *ratzach*, which refers not to killing as such, but to the deliberate, unlawful taking of innocent human life. Therefore the sixth commandment prohibits murder. While all murder is killing not all killing is murder. As a matter of fact, the same divinely revealed legal code that proscribes "Ratsach" (murder) prescribes death as the penalty for breaking that

---

[6] All scripture quotations are taken from the New American Standard Bible version unless otherwise indicated.

7

law (Exodus 21:12). So the sixth commandment cannot logically prohibit all killing under any circumstances. Obviously, God did not forbid his people to kill under any circumstance and then command them to execute those who broke that commandment.

Therefore, while this scripture does not establish a Biblical foundation for the use of lethal force in self-defense per se, the proper understanding of this scripture does serve to remove a common barrier to legitimizing the use of lethal force in self-defense; that barrier being the false impression that the sixth commandment forbids all killing.

In addition, this commandment, coupled with the penalty of capital punishment for its violation (Exodus 21:12), helps to establish the high value that God places upon human life. Your life is your most precious gift from God. God demands the forfeiture of the life of anyone who "steals" your life via murder. God does not demand "gold for life" or "cattle for life" but "life for life." Wouldn't it logically follow that, when necessary, God would permit you to use deadly force to prevent your murder from occurring in the first place? The next passage would seem to so indicate.

2) **Exodus 22:2-3 "If the thief is caught while breaking in and is struck so that he dies, there will be no bloodguiltiness on his account. But if the sun has risen on him, there will be bloodguiltiness on his account. He shall surely make restitution; if he owns nothing, then he shall be sold for his theft."**

What does this scripture passage teach us about the use of lethal force in personal self-defense? There are two contrasting scenarios pictured in these verses. In the first, the thief is **"caught while breaking in."** In the second, he is caught after **"the sun has risen on him."** The assumption seems to be that in the first scenario the thief broke in at night i.e. before the **"sun has risen on him."**

Thus, if the thief is caught "in the act" so to speak, and confronted by the homeowner while breaking in at night, and the homeowner uses force to defend himself, and that force results in the death of the thief, the owner is not guilty of murder, **"there will be no bloodguiltiness on his account."** If, however, the thief escapes, and is later found by the homeowner, i.e. after **"the sun has risen on him"**, and the homeowner then kills the thief, it would be considered murder, **"there will be bloodguiltiness on his account."**

In other words, this Old Testament law is specifying that lethal force is permitted the individual when his life is threatened, such as in a home invasion in the dead of night, presumably because in that situation there are no reasonable alternatives to the use of force. The surprised homeowner under assault cannot call the police (if there were such a thing in ancient Israel). The homeowner cannot know whether the motive and intention of the intruder is solely larcenous or also homicidal. The homeowner has neither the time nor the opportunity to divine those motives and so must assume the worst. The homeowner is in a desperate "kill or be killed" situation. Therefore, the circumstances are such that he may justifiably use lethal force against the intruder in order to safeguard the precious gift of life with which God has entrusted him.

However, the morning after a break-in and robbery, the justifiability of the use of lethal force is completely altered in that there is no immediate threat to the life of the homeowner. The homeowner now has alternatives to the personal use of force to defend his life, family and property. The homeowner has the option, and therefore the obligation, to involve the civil authorities in their role of law enforcement in the name of justice. The homeowner is not free to go out in the cold light of day to hunt down the thief and kill him. If he does then **"there will be bloodguiltiness on his account."** The thief is now known to be a thief only and not a murderer. The proper penalty is restitution not execution. In the "day after" scenario the homeowner must let the civil authorities step in to apprehend the thief, assess the appropriate penalties, and compel restitution. Again, **"the sun having risen"** indicates the thief being found at some later time rather than while he was in the process of breaking in as in the first scenario.

In this law God seems to recognize mitigating circumstances justifying the personal use of force, even lethal force, by an individual. Those circumstances include an immediate threat to the individual's life or his family's life, the absence of state protection, and the lack of reasonable alternatives to escape or retreat.

This law also establishes a use of force that does not fit neatly into the categories of vengeance or retribution. That category is "self-defense." An individual who uses force to disrupt a violent attack in progress upon himself or his family is not being vengeful. He is not "paying back" the attacker for what he has done. He does not necessarily hate his attacker. He is not necessarily angry with his attacker. He may very well be motivated by nothing more than a legitimate desire to prevent the execution of a violent act upon himself or others.

Some have attributed the ultimate motive of love to the legitimate use of force by the state. Jack Cottrell writes, *"The main point of the just war is not to maim or kill the enemy, but to protect the innocent and law-abiding. What is this but an expression of neighbor-love?"*[7] Indeed! It is therefore no stretch to ascribe the same motivation of "neighbor-love" to the individual in desperate circumstances trying to protect the lives of her children. This scripture appears to make that very distinction!

3) **Esther 8:11** **"The king granted the Jews who were in**

---

[7] Cottrell

each and every city the right to assemble and to defend their lives."

The context of this passage has the Jews living in exile in Persia. A wicked man named Haman manipulated the king into passing a law declaring that on a certain day it would be "open season" on the Jews; the Persians could attack, kill and despoil them without any legal repercussions. Later, when the king realized that Haman had manipulated him, he passed a second law granting the Jews the right to defend themselves from the scheduled attack. This they proceeded to do with extreme prejudice! **Esther 9:5 "Thus the Jews struck all their enemies with the sword, killing and destroying; and they did what they pleased to those who hated them."**

Note that this was not a Jewish militia, army or police force doing battle with the enemies of Israel. These were the ordinary private Jewish citizens who had armed themselves and who successfully used lethal force in their own defense. The Old Testament did not restrict the legitimate use of force to the state.

The Jewish feast of Purim commemorates these events and is still celebrated to this day. It is a Jewish feast that commemorates, in part, the right to self-defense. A modern-day parallel might be Americans having a National holiday called "Stand Your Ground" day.

Granted, strictly speaking, in this case the law empowering the Jews to employ lethal force in self-defense was not an oracle of God - it came from a pagan king. God's name is not even mentioned in the book of Esther. However, God's purpose for including this book in the Old Testament canon seems to be a witness to his protecting providence as well as an explanation of the origin of the feast of Purim. That being the case, we infer God's approval of the Jewish actions in defending themselves. This, then, represents God's approval of personal self-defense.

4) **Nehemiah 4:14, 17, 20b** **"(14) When I saw their fear, I rose and spoke to the nobles, the officials and the rest of the people: 'Do not be afraid of them; remember the Lord who is great and awesome, and fight for your brothers, your sons, your daughters, your wives and your houses.' (17) Those who were rebuilding the wall and those who carried burdens took their load with one hand doing the work and the other holding a weapon. (20b) 'Our God will fight for us.'"**

The context of this passage has Nehemiah returning to Israel from Persian exile to lead the effort to rebuild the walls of Jerusalem. There is stiff and violent opposition to his efforts from the locals and so he commands each citizen-laborer to arm himself for self-defense. Later on, Nehemiah says that they wore their weapons continuously (Nehemiah 4:23). Note several important points about armed self-defense from this passage.

First, this is not the state government "bearing the sword" in its God-given judicial role of enforcing justice for the citizenry ala Romans 13:4. That is a primary function of government but that's not what is being described here. As in the example of Esther, these are private Jewish citizens who are being encouraged to carry weapons for self-defense.

Secondly, they were told to fight for their families and their homes. This represents the use of deadly force to defend life and property.

Thirdly, Nehemiah said, **"Our God will fight for us" (Nehemiah 4:20)** but notice that their reliance upon God to "fight for" them did not preclude the necessity that they defend themselves. Some might suggest that trusting in God's protection is co-equal with personal disarmament and passivity in the face of violent criminal attack. Such a view is contradicted by this passage. Arming for self-defense, training for self-defense, and acting in self-defense are not mutually exclusive with reliance upon God to "fight for us."

We could multiply examples of the foundational right to self-defense set forth in the Old Testament but please allow these to suffice. We will now move on to look at some of the relevant New Testament scriptures. If you are a Christian then your primary rule of faith and practice is found in the New Covenant Scriptures. However, let us acknowledge that even for New Testament Christians the foundational principles of self-defense drawn from the Old Testament are still relevant. Paul's attitude toward the events recorded in the Old Testament should be our attitude as well, i.e. learn from them. **I Corinthians 10:11 "Now these things happened to them as an example, and they were written for our instruction, upon whom the ends of the ages have come."**

Old Testament principles such as the immorality of murder and the right to self-defense are still valid and have never been abrogated by God in the New Testament, as we shall see.

PART TWO

A NEW TESTAMENT THEOLOGY
OF SELF-DEFENSE

1. SELF-DEFENSE AND THE EXAMPLE OF JESUS

Did Jesus ever defend himself from a violent attack or from an attempt on his life? Did Jesus ever defend others from violent attacks or attempts on their lives? Did Jesus ever use force or any of his special powers in his defense or in the defense of others? The answer to the questions above is "yes." That might sound surprising. Those familiar with the gospel records will undoubtedly remember that when the soldiers came to arrest Jesus he did not resist. When they beat him and crucified him he did not defend himself. It is true that Jesus offered no physical resistance at his arrest and crucifixion. The arrest and crucifixion of Jesus were all part of the preordained plan of God (Acts 2:23). When Jesus surrendered himself to the violent intentions of those men it was a great act of physical, emotional and spiritual courage as well as obedience to the Father. In the Garden of Gethsemane, it was finally time for Jesus to voluntarily and intentionally sacrifice himself on behalf of others, but what about before that time? Consider the following examples of Jesus practicing self-defense.

1) <u>Luke 4:28-29</u> **"And all the people in the synagogue were filled with rage as they heard these things; and they got up and drove Jesus out of the city, and led Him to the brow of the hill on which their city had been built, in order to throw Him down the cliff. But passing through their midst, He went His way."**

This was an angry, violent mob. This mob was trying to kill Jesus. They attacked Jesus and forcibly drove him out of the city to the edge of a cliff. They were going to throw him off the cliff to his death on the rocks below. But Jesus didn't let them do that. Jesus defended his life and refused to let this mob have their way with him. Is this an example of self-defense by Jesus? Yes it is! Did he use force to defend himself? No, he did not. What did he use? We do not know. Apparently he employed some aspect of his divine powers to simply walk right through the crowd and go on his way. We can't defend ourselves in the same way because we don't have that particular power but Jesus could and he did. My point is that Jesus defended himself against those who wanted to kill him. He was perfectly willing to die when the appointed time came, but he wasn't ready or willing to die at this particular time. He did not respond to this violent attack with passive non-resistance. He did not let others kill him just because they wanted to. He resisted.

2) <u>John 10:31, 39</u> **"The Jews picked up stones again to stone him...therefore they were seeking again to seize him, and he eluded their grasp."**

This is a very similar incident where a violent mob was intent on killing Jesus. In this case, they weren't going to kill him by throwing him off a cliff; they were going to kill him by pelting him with stones. Once again, Jesus was having none of it. Perhaps he did the same thing here that he did before at the cliff - he simply slipped on his "invisibility cloak" and walked right through them, we do not know. By whatever means, he refused to let them

16

have their way with him. It wasn't time.

So we see clearly that Jesus did use his powers to defend his own life from violent attack on at least two occasions. Is a follower of Christ permitted to follow his Lord's example in this respect? The next time someone makes an attempt on your life and you glance at your WWJD bracelet and ask yourself, "What would Jesus do?" I suggest that the answer may very well be to resist. Now let us see how Jesus defended others from violence.

3) In **John 8:1-11** Jesus personally saved a woman from death by stoning at the hands of a Jewish mob. In that instance he did not use force or supernatural power to save her life. Employing his verbal skills to defuse the volatile situation Jesus saved the desperate woman from a brutal and gruesome fate. What if Jesus had not succeeded in disarming the murderous mob with his words? Would he have simply squatted on the sidelines, scratching in the dust with his finger while this woman was executed before his very eyes? We do not know. We might speculate that based upon what we know of his character, his actions, and his tendency to defend the helpless, it is reasonable to assume that Jesus would have escalated his efforts to rescue this woman's life. Regardless, this much is certain; in this account Jesus defended the woman and, in so doing, saved her life.

4) In **Acts 9:1-19** the Jewish Pharisee Saul was on his way to Damascus in order to arrest and imprison Christians. Jesus intercepted him on the road and blinded him. In the long-term this confrontation led to the conversion of Saul to Christianity. In the short term this confrontation resulted in the deliverance of untold innocent Christians from confiscation of private property, imprisonment and death. And once again for the record, just how did Jesus disrupt Saul's violent rampage? Jesus confronted Saul and blinded him. Blinding someone is a pretty extreme

measure by most any standard. Granted, he didn't use pepper spray or mace - he used the brilliant light of his glorious presence. You do what works best for you. I'm sure that once those Christians in Damascus who had been on Saul's "hit list" found out about this intervention, they were very grateful for Jesus' use of force on their behalf.

5) Luke 22:35-36 "And Jesus said to them, 'When I sent you out without money belt and bag and sandals, you did not lack anything, did you?' They said, 'No, nothing.' And He said to them, 'But now, whoever has a money belt is to take it along, likewise also a bag, and whoever has no sword is to sell his coat and buy one.'"

When Jesus sent out his disciples on their first training exercise without Him (Matthew 10), he told them to take no supplies with them. However, the Lord's instructions on the eve of His trial reveal the earlier instructions as a special circumstance, not standard operating policy; now, they are to use the resources they have. The money belt, bag and sandals are still optional. However, the disciples are each ordered to acquire swords for their journey, even if they have to sell their coats to get one. That's like Jesus coming to your church today and saying, "All right Christians, I expect each of you to go out and buy a Glock. If you can't afford one then hold a yard sale to raise the money." Scholars and commentators are divided regarding the implications of this instruction from Jesus but this much we know for certain, on this occasion Jesus instructed his disciples to arm themselves with swords.

6) When Jesus was arrested in the Garden of Gethsemane, Peter whipped out his sword and cut off the ear of one of the men in the mob. What did Jesus do? He reattached the ear and said to Peter, **"Put the sword into the sheath; the cup which the Father has given me, shall I not drink it" (John 18:11).** He did not say, "Throw that

sword away and renounce all violence." He just said to put it back in its sheath. In today's parlance Jesus might say, "Reholster your Glock, Peter." Why didn't Jesus permit Peter and the other disciples to resist with their swords? For the same reason that Jesus himself did not resist at this time; this was the time and place when Jesus chose to die. But make no mistake - this was Jesus' deliberate choice to fulfill his mission. It was not his passive submission to an unforeseen criminal attack. In his three-year ministry Jesus had already demonstrated his inclination to defend himself rather than let thugs take his life at their whim.

7) **John 18:6-9** **"So when He said to them, 'I am He,' they drew back and fell to the ground. Therefore He again asked them, 'Whom do you seek?' And they said, 'Jesus the Nazarene.' Jesus answered, 'I told you that I am He; so if you seek me, let these go their way,' to fulfill the word which He spoke, 'Of those whom you have given me I lost not one.'"**

Here we see another example of Jesus' disposition (and example) to defend others. Why did Jesus seek to save the lives of his disciples when he was arrested? Was it just to fulfill his prophetic pronouncement, "Of those whom you have given me I lost not one"? What was the sentiment behind that pronouncement? The sentiment was love for his disciples coupled with a desire to protect them and save their lives. These men were his spiritual family. He wanted to protect them just like you want to protect your family...and he did protect them just as you do protect yours, and rightly so.

Why did the Roman cohort and officers from the chief priests and Pharisees follow Jesus' instructions and let the disciples go? Why didn't they arrest the disciples, especially after Peter's sword attack on the high priest's servant? Perhaps it is because Jesus had already blown them all down to the ground in some mysterious manner (John 18:6). Could that use of force have something to do with the suddenly cooperative spirit of the mob to do what Jesus told them? Could that have something to do with Jesus' successful defense of the disciples?

8) Finally, the New Testament records incidents wherein Jesus, John the Baptist and the Apostles interacted with and evangelized members of the military (**Luke 3:14, Matthew 8:10, & Acts 10**). There is no record of a single instance wherein those in the military were instructed to resign their commission, lay down their arms and/or become pacifists in order to enter the Kingdom of God. This is not a specific affirmation of the legitimacy of individual self-defense per se since soldiers are a part of the state government. However, these interactions do reinforce my central argument in that they imply there is no inherent contradiction between discipleship and the legitimate use of lethal force.

The example and teaching of Jesus in the above passages affirms the following:
1) The right to self-defense.
2) The right to carry a weapon for self-defense.
3) By implication, the right to use lethal force in self-defense.
4) Jesus' disposition and willingness to intercede, by force if necessary, to rescue the weak and helpless who were threatened with deadly violence.
5) Jesus' disposition and willingness to intervene on behalf of his spiritual family to shield them from violence.

2. SELF-DEFENSE AND THE NEW TESTAMENT DOCTRINE OF STEWARDSHIP

You are responsible to God for your life. The Bible teaches that God **"gives life to all things" (I Timothy 6:13)**. Your life, therefore, is a gift from God and, strictly speaking, is not your own. Not only has God created you and given you the gift of life, but he has a second claim on your life by virtue of redemption: **I Corinthians 6:19-20**

"You are not your own for you have been bought with a price." So let us acknowledge that in the ultimate sense we owe our lives to God. Having said that, however, there is a sense in which God has entrusted to us *relative* ownership and control of our lives. That is, within the framework of God's general will revealed in his written word, we have the right, and even the obligation, to control, protect, defend and conduct our own lives. This principle is known as stewardship.

In **John 10:18** Jesus stated, **"No one has taken my life away from me, but I lay it down on my own initiative. I have authority to lay it down, and I have authority to take it up again. This commandment I received from My Father."** Jesus did not consider himself to be at the mercy of the criminal element of his day. They wanted to take his life and attempted to do so on more than one occasion. But he was in control of his own life. He might choose to lay it down at some point but that would be his choice and on his terms. As we have seen, no one laid a hand on Jesus until he was ready. Even when Jesus was killed his life was not "taken" it was "given." God had given him this authority regarding the stewardship of his Earthly life.

God has given you a similar authority regarding the stewardship of your life. Admittedly, we do not exercise the comprehensive control over our lives that Jesus did over his. As the Son of God Jesus literally controlled all contingencies and circumstances and was therefore able to choose the time and manner of his death (in concert with the prophecies that had been made him). Obviously, as finite creatures there are many contingencies and circumstances in life that we do not control. We have little to no control over hurricanes, tornados, earthquakes, lightening strikes, flash floods, congenital heart defects, most diseases, airplane accidents, and the like. We might take what we believe to be every reasonable precaution to protect our lives and still wind up dying "prematurely" through some unforeseeable eventuality. That's why we must qualify any discussion of the concept of "control" over our lives as relative control.

With that being said, however, we do exercise a relative control over the gift of life with which God has entrusted us. You are a steward of the life that God has given to you. Until the day you die your life remains under your control and you have the right, and even the obligation, to defend your life and to spend your life in accordance with God's will. In fact, of all the gifts that God has entrusted to you as a steward, none is more valuable than your life. That is why the greatest act of love possible is to lay down ones life for his friends (John 15:13). Therefore the choices we make regarding the defense, protection and sacrifice of life are of great consequence. But beneath the general umbrella of God's will as expressed in his Word, those choices are your choices to make - not someone else's. Nowhere does God's word obligate you to forfeit your gift of life to someone else, just because that person has a malicious, illegal and immoral desire to rob you of your life.

Someone might argue that the teachings of Jesus warning us not to cling to our lives too jealously preclude the use of lethal force to defend our lives. Consider the following examples.

Luke 9:24 "For whoever wishes to save his life will lose it, but whoever loses his life for my sake, he is the one who will save it."

Luke 14:26 "If anyone comes to Me, and does not hate his own father and mother and wife and children and brothers and sisters, yes, and even his own life, he cannot be My disciple."

John 12:25 "He who loves his life loses it, and he who hates his life in this world will keep it to life eternal."

But in these verses Jesus is not teaching us to devalue "life." Rather he is teaching us to reorder our value system so that we prioritize that which will result in eternal life.

We are not to be so absorbed in and obsessed with the cares of this temporal, earthly phase of our lives that we neglect and devalue the spiritual things of the Kingdom. So **"losing your life"** and **"hating your life"** do not justify killing yourself, abusing yourself, acting recklessly with regard to your safety and well being, or passively submitting yourself to die at the hands of a criminal. None of that is incorporated into the context of these verses or others like them. Rather "losing your life" and "hating your life" refer to the attitude of faith that says nothing this life has to offer me is more important, valuable, or worthwhile than Jesus and his kingdom. As Paul writes in **Galatians 2:20** **"I have been crucified with Christ; and it is no longer I who live, but Christ lives in me; and the life which I now live in the flesh I live by faith in the Son of God, who loved me and gave Himself up for me."**

3. SELF-DEFENSE AND THE NEW TESTAMENT DOCTRINE OF MANHOOD
I Timothy 5:8 **"But if anyone does not provide for his own, and especially for those of his household, he has denied the faith and is worse than an unbeliever."**

The modern church is becoming increasingly feminized. The percentage of men participating in church grows smaller each year. The typical US worship service draws an adult crowd that's 61 percent women. Church volunteers and employees are overwhelmingly female. Major national men's ministries such as Promise Keepers used to pack stadiums–but now have trouble filling church auditoriums. Ethnic and overseas churches report gender gaps as high as 10 to 1. Christian colleges are becoming convents. Men are the world's largest unreached people group.

What has caused the feminization of the church? There are many historical/cultural causes for what we are seeing today but I would suggest that one of those causes is the church's position on this issue of self-defense. Pacifism does not appeal to men. Men intuitively sense that they are responsible to provide for their wives and children and that "protection" is encompassed in that provision. These men are right. A man's intuitive sense of responsibility to protect his family from the violent attack of criminal predators is there because God has written it on his heart and commanded it in his Word. **Malachi 2:16 "'The man who hates and divorces his wife,' says the Lord, the God of Israel, 'does violence to the one he should protect,' says the Lord Almighty".**[8] God says that a man's wife is **"the one he should protect."** One of the problems with divorce, at least in ancient Israelite culture, was that it exposed a man's dependents to criminal violence. A man's wife is his "dependent" in the sense that she depends upon her husband for protection.

God's charge of protection is clearly laid at the feet of the husband, the father, the man of the house. My point here is not that women cannot defend themselves and their families. They can, they did, they do and they should. My point is that God's Word seems to lay the greater responsibility for protection upon the men.

When Christian preachers, teachers, writers and bloggers suggest that the proper posture of Christian men is pacifism, or even semi-pacifism, the appeal of Christianity to men is seriously diminished. If you tell a man that once he becomes a Christian he is not permitted to defend his life from a thug, home-invader, crack-head or gang-banger you have just told him something that goes against his God-given sense of dignity, self-worth and justice. When you tell that man that not only is he not permitted to defend himself, but he is also not permitted to use force to protect his wife from a rapist or his children from a kidnapper, child-molester, or pedophile, you will have told him something that contradicts what

---

[8] Holy Bible, New International Version, http://www.biblegateway.com

God has written on his heart. You have just emasculated that man.

I'm not suggesting that all, or even most churches, currently teach pacifism, they don't. I'm suggesting that most churches generally don't teach anything at all about self-defense. They say little to nothing about the protection aspect of a man's provision for his family. How many sermons have you heard (or preached) about Christian self-defense? How many books have you read about Christian self-defense? That silence on the subject is almost as bad as actively teaching pacifism. By remaining silent on this topic preachers reinforce the "default" position lurking in the collective sub-conscious of the modern traditional church and that default position is pacifism. By remaining silent about the legitimacy of Christian self-defense and family protection the Church unnecessarily undermines its evangelism and conservation of men. In the first century, the Apostle Paul fought against the idea that men had to first become Jews before they could become Christians. In this century we must fight against the idea that men must first become women before they can become Christians.

4. SELF-DEFENSE AND THE NEW TESTAMENT DOCTRINE OF MISSIONS

The Apostle Paul was the first Christian missionary. He was probably the most effective Christian missionary in all of history. One of the overlooked factors contributing to Paul's success as a missionary is Paul's protection. God providentially and miraculously protected Paul's life. In recounting his confrontation with Jesus on the road to Damascus Paul reveals Jesus' explicit determination to personally guard Paul's life until his missionary activities were completed.

Acts 26:15-18 **"'I am Jesus, whom you are persecuting,' the Lord replied. 'Now get up and stand on your feet. I have appeared to you to appoint**

you as a servant and as a witness of what you have seen and will see of me. *I will rescue you from your own people and from the Gentiles.* I am sending you to them to open their eyes and turn them from darkness to light, and from the power of Satan to God, so that they may receive forgiveness of sins and a place among those who are sanctified by faith in me.'"

Jesus promised to rescue Paul as he conducted his missionary activities. I would suggest that this is an overlooked and under-utilized principle of missions. Call it "protected evangelism." Granted, Paul was not protected to the degree that he never suffered harm, quite the contrary. Paul was among the most beaten and battered soldiers of Christ you will ever read of. But God protected his life so that he could spread the word. Seven times in the book of Acts we read of God rescuing, delivering, reviving or protecting Paul's life in his missionary endeavors. Three of those times of deliverance were providential: Acts 14:5-7, Acts 21:30-32, and Acts 23:12-24. Four of those times of deliverance were miraculous: Acts 14:19-20, Acts 16:25-37, Acts 27:23-26, and Acts 28:3-6.

Jesus followed through on his promise of protection for Paul. Why did Jesus protect Paul in his missionary activities? Obviously, if God's messenger is killed then the message is hindered. As Paul wrote in **Romans 10:14** **"How can they hear without someone preaching to them? And how can anyone preach unless they are sent?"** I would add, "And how can they hear the preacher who was sent if he is killed en route?"

My premise is simple, Jesus' providential and supernatural protection for Paul as a missionary is a Biblical precedent of protection for Christians to follow today. Just as we look at Jesus' miraculous feeding of the five thousand and follow his lead by our non-miraculous feeding of the poor and hungry. Just as we look at Jesus' miraculous healing of the sick and follow his lead by our non-miraculous ministrations to those who are sick. So likewise we can look at Jesus' miraculous protection for missionaries and follow his lead by our non-miraculous protection for missionaries in hostile fields.

Christian persecution is on the rise in our world. Christian populations are being systematically exterminated in many places. Seemingly, the only counter-measures ever suggested by Christian leaders and human rights activists are the "same old, same old" pacifist or semi-pacifist clichés. For instance, John L. Allen Jr. is the author of "The Global War on Christians." When asked how Western Churches can best help persecuted Christians and churches around the world he responded, *"There are plenty of things to be done, from prayer to humanitarian relief to consciousness-raising. When I ask persecuted Christians this question, however, the first thing they always say is, 'Don't forget about us.' They have a powerful sense of having been abandoned and ignored, which exacerbates their hardships. The best answer to what Western churches can do, therefore, is to make it clear in every way possible that they haven't forgotten."*[9] While this advice is fine as far as it goes, it doesn't go far enough. Isn't there at least one more action that Western Churches and some of those persecuted churches can take? They can take the action of protection. Why not teach the Christians in Pakistan, Nigeria, Libya, Syria and Kenya that God wants them to defend their lives, their families and their churches from frenzied Muslim attackers? Why not post an armed guard in the persecuted church on Sunday? Many American churches are already deploying armed security for Sunday services and in some cases this defensive measure has already saved Christian lives. When Christian lives are saved then Christian ground is held, Christian ground that has been hard-won by the efforts of missionaries and

---

[9]   www.christianpost.com/news/the-global-war-on-christians-is-the-unreported-catastrophe-of-our-time-author-argues-108871 (November 15, 2013)

evangelists in their attempts to advance the Kingdom of God.

Note that "protected evangelism" as herein advocated is not violent aggression any more than personal self-defense is revenge or punishment. We are not talking about the misguided policy of using violence to subjugate a people so that they can then have Christianity forcibly shoved down their throats. Christians evangelize via persuasion in the arena of ideas. We simply need to survive long enough to get the message out!

5. SELF-DEFENSE AND THE NEW TESTAMENT DOCTRINE OF RESTRAINT

But what of Jesus' famous teaching in the Sermon on the Mount to "turn the other cheek?" Most of the Christian angst regarding self-defense arises from two verses in the New Testament: **Matthew 5:38-39 "You have heard that it was said, 'An eye for an eye, and a tooth for a tooth.' But I say to you, do not resist an evil person; but whoever slaps you on your right cheek; turn the other to him also."** If not for those two verses it is doubtful that sincere followers of Christ would ever seriously question the Biblical principle of self-defense so clearly and thoroughly delineated in the rest of scripture. So let us turn our attention to this important passage.

There are two primary views among scholars regarding Jesus' "Turn the other cheek" instruction. The pacifist view maintains that Jesus was introducing a new and total prohibition against the use of force by his followers, even for the purpose of self-defense. The other view maintains that Jesus was correcting the misapplication of Old Testament principle by the Pharisees. He was therefore instructing his followers to practice self-restraint in the face of an insult. He was not prohibiting self-defense in the face of a violent attack. Both views have been thoroughly expounded over the years by scholars in countless Bible commentaries. I embrace and recommend the latter view and will summarize it here.

The context of "turn the other cheek" is a discourse by Jesus on the Old Testament Law of Moses. This discourse takes place within the larger context of the Sermon on the Mount contained in Matthew chapters 5-7. The fact that the scribes and Pharisees misunderstood the requirements and intentions of the Law of Moses underlies Jesus' statement earlier in the sermon, **Matthew 5:20 "For I say to you that unless your righteousness surpasses that of the scribes and Pharisees, you will not enter the kingdom of heaven."** Over the years the Law of Moses had been twisted and watered down by the scribes and Pharisees of Jesus' day. They were way off target in their ideas of following the Law (see Matthew 15:1-3). They were so far off that they gave equal authority to their traditions, and some of them actually thought that they were keeping the righteous requirements of the Law by their outward show of religiosity. In order to correct these wrong views Jesus selected six areas of the Law of Moses, which had been misinterpreted through the oral tradition of the scribes and Pharisees. These areas are covered in Matthew 5:21-48 and include murder, adultery, divorce, vows, retaliation and neighbor relations. It is significant that Jesus does not begin His comments on each of the six areas with the words, "It is written…" but rather with the words, "You have heard that it was said…" (Vs. 21, 27, 31, 33, 38, and 43). This indicates that it was not just the particular Old Testament Scripture that Jesus had in mind but the wrong ideas that had built up around that Scripture as well.

In Matthew 5:38-39 Jesus deals with what has become known as the lex talionis (law of retaliation). The scribes and Pharisees had taken this area of the Civil Law and twisted it to justify selfish acts of personal vengeance. God never gave "An eye for an eye, and a tooth for a tooth" as a guideline for personal vengeance and retaliation. Each time this law is mentioned in the Old Testament (Exodus 21:24; Leviticus 24:20; Deuteronomy 19:21) the context is civil justice–not individual "tit-for-tat". "Let the punishment fit the crime" was God's directive for civil law and order. But over the years this law was increasingly misinterpreted and used by the scribes and Pharisees to carry on their personal vendettas. So Jesus issued a corrective in **Matthew 5:39 "Do not resist an evil person; but whoever slaps you on your right cheek; turn the other to him also."** In Jesus' culture, to be struck on the right cheek was to be given a hostile, backhanded insult. This is a pivotal interpretive issue. The circumstance that Jesus was teaching to was not a violent, life-threatening attack but a personal, humiliating insult. The teaching is that when a Christ-follower is insulted he is to exercise self-restraint and non-retaliation out of love. Not only are we not to overreact when insulted, we are not even to retaliate in kind. There is no place for an attitude of "I'll get you back" or "Wait 'till I get my hands on you." When someone takes advantage of us, insults us, talks behind our back or excludes us, we are to "turn the other cheek" and not retaliate even though it may hurt us (Mt.5:39), cost us (Mt.5:40), inconvenience us (Mt.5:41), or exhaust us (Mt.5:42).

Hermeneutics is the science of interpreting scripture. I believe the "restraint-in-the-face-of-insult" interpretation of Matthew 5:39 is hermeneutically sound because it:

a) Takes into account the immediate problem of the Pharisaical misuse of scripture alluded to in the larger portion of the discourse (the hermeneutical principle of context), and

b) Raises no barriers to the right to self-defense established in the Old Testament scriptures and in the example of Jesus' own life (the hermeneutical principle of harmonization).

PART THREE

THE PRACTICAL APPLICATION OF
TURNING THE OTHER CHEEK

The practical result of applying such a policy of restraint-in-the-face-of-insult in our conduct toward others is, in a word, peace. Anyone who takes this higher road will be far more likely in his everyday life to avoid much unnecessary grief, drama and potentially violent conflict. All you have to sacrifice in return is a little bit of pride. Allow me to submit just two true-life examples to illustrate. Author John Caile, writing in Concealed Carry Magazine, provides the first example.

In June of 2007, a 32-year-old security employee and carry permit holder (whom we will call "Todd") was in an SUV with his wife sitting next to him, and his two young children in back. Todd was stopped behind several cars at a red light, when he glanced at the side-view mirror on his wife's side of the car. Todd noticed a Monte Carlo somewhere back in the line of traffic pull out onto the right hand shoulder of the road, pass all of the cars, then pull in front of the lead car and run right through the red light.

When the Monte Carlo passed his SUV, what should Todd have done? How about nothing? Why not just ignore the incident? Unfortunately, that was not what he did.

Todd could have simply called 911 and reported the vehicle running a red light. But Todd didn't do that either.

Like too many people today, Todd seemed to think it was his job to let another driver know what he thought of his driving. As the Monte Carlo passed his SUV, Todd leaned on his horn, stuck his left hand out of his window and flipped off the other driver, setting in motion events that would alter his life forever.

As it turned out, the driver of the Monte Carlo had heard the horn, turned his head and saw Todd's gesture. After running the red light, he pulled off to the side of the road and waited for the line of cars (including Todd) to catch up. He then pulled in behind the other cars.

At the next light, which was red, Todd was stopped behind a car in the middle lane. The right lane was "Right Turn Only" and the Monte Carlo pulled up and stopped on the right hand side of Todd's SUV. The driver waved a gun out the window at Todd's wife, and yelled, "You (expletive deleted!) I'll kill you, and I don't even care about jail!"

Rather odd comment, wasn't it? More on that later. Todd saw a guy with a gun threatening to kill him, so he pulled his own handgun, leaned across in front of his wife and fired twice. The light changed to green, Todd took off and his wife called 911. They then pulled into a gas station a few blocks down and waited for the police.

Meanwhile, the driver of the Monte Carlo had been hit, a minor wound in his thigh, but he, too made a 911 call. It went like this:

911 Operator: *"Nine-one-one, what's your emergency?"*

Monte Carlo Driver: *"Officer down!"*

That's right, Todd had shot an off-duty, undercover, narcotics detective. I have a question for you: How do you think this is going to work out for our friend, Todd?

By the way, how many cops do you think showed up after that call? All of them would be pretty close - 12 cars from four different agencies.

Now guess which of these two gentlemen wound up in a police car in handcuffs. That would be Todd, of course.

In a perfect world, Todd would still probably have been in trouble but the police officer would also have been charged with at least making a terroristic threat, if not second degree assault with a deadly weapon.

But we don't live in a perfect world. Todd was arrested, got out on bail the next day, and when he showed up for work and explained his absence he was immediately fired. No security company is going to keep an employee who just shot a cop - regardless of the circumstances.

Finally, in 2009, after two years of legal wrangling, Todd had to plead guilty to felony negligent discharge of a firearm. He got 60 days in jail, and as a convicted felon, lost his right to vote and to own firearms of any kind. Perhaps worst of all, his employment prospects will now be considerably limited...for the rest of his life.

And the cop? The state's attorney declined to prosecute. But even more outrageously, the officer was given a commendation for "being wounded on duty" in spite of the fact that he was suspected of slacking (not working) at the time of the incident. Now you know why he didn't "care about jail."

"Not fair!" you say. Maybe. But Todd had a choice. All he had to do when he saw that guy driving down the shoulder of the road was ignore him. But instead, Todd just had to lean on that horn and give him the finger. To his lifelong regret.

Now think of all the people you might run into - meth heads, gangbangers, and drug dealers. The list is endless. You really have no idea who you're about to provoke. So do yourself (and the rest of us) a favor. Drive courteously. Never flip off anyone. Ever. No tailgating. No flashing your lights. Someone's coming down the ramp to merge? Slow down and let them in, or move over if you can. Someone doesn't take their turn at the four-way stop? So what? Let it go. There is no upside to leaning on your horn or giving someone the finger. But the downside could be disastrous. Just ask Todd.[10]

The second true-life example is taken from self-defense instructor Tim Larkin's book, "How To Survive The Most Critical Five Seconds of Your Life."

"Here's a classic example of a trained reaction to avoidable

---

[10] John Caile, "Concealed Carry Magazine," May/June 2013.

violence. Matt, one of my Mastery students posted this sad story on our Target Focused Training (TFT) Mastery Forum:

In Dallas we have a famous little nightspot called the Gypsy Tea Room. You can see acts like Ben Harper, Edie Brickel, Old 97's, etc.

Recently, a father of two teenage girls decided to take his daughters to an end-of-summer show before they left for college. Before the show was over he ended up having a severed spinal cord injury and can feel nothing from the neck down. Why? Needless social violence.

He engaged a 'skinhead' in a verbal altercation because the skinhead made a comment to one of his daughters. This led to male posturing, yelling, etc. And then the skinhead opened his 'toolbox of violence' first and pummeled the guy to the floor.

As the father was on the floor the skinhead stomped down on his face and severed the man's spinal cord somewhere between the C-1 and C-5. This all occurred right in front of his two daughters.

Situations like this remind me of the many reasons why I thank God TFT came into my life. Why? Most people would think that I would say because if I were this father I would have kicked the skinhead's ass because of my training. WRONG.

Because of what I have learned from TFT I would not have engaged the skinhead in any verbal altercation. If the skinhead tried to start a verbal altercation I would have gotten my girls and myself out of the club immediately. All the while trying to look the coward - the wimp.

Don't get me wrong; if the situation were going to become violent I would have made it very violent. But, more than likely, simply leaving the club would have saved this man a lifetime of paralysis and spared his daughters from witnessing a horrific act."[11]

What is Tim Larkin's philosophy of dealing with personal insults? *"Personally, I've found I'm much more likely to capitulate and disengage by leaving the area, without a word, when*

---

[11] Tim Larkin, "How to Survive the Most Critical Five Seconds of Your Life," (Vervante April 11, 2012) page 35-36

confronted by someone with an obvious chip on their shoulder who has chosen me as the knock-off guy. Everybody wins - I sleep well and he doesn't get a broken leg just because he was having a bad day. I find that I am possessed of a saint-like patience these days - somewhere, somehow I developed the habit of giving pretty much everyone the benefit of the doubt. I do not begrudge those who are curt and prickly their public anger and annoyance. I just figure there are extenuating circumstances I'm not aware of and I have no desire to be the next point on the down trending curve of their bad day. I do my best to treat everyone with patience and respect."[12]

Jesus' admonition to "turn the other cheek" does not preclude self-defense, but that doesn't mean that Christians should go to the opposite extreme of looking for trouble. It is inappropriate for Christians to swagger around alert for opportunities to open up a can of "Old Testament wrath" on anyone who looks at us sideways. Turning the other cheek is the most powerful path to the avoidance of violent conflict ever verbalized. And it's notable that many modern-day experts in self-defense and reality-based combat have come to the same conclusions.

So, when do you defend yourself and when do you turn the other cheek? This is a question of discernment. You must discern between two very different types of situations. The following apocryphal story may help to enlighten.

In 1986, Mkele Mbembe was on holiday in Kenya after graduating from Northwestern University. On a hike through the brush, he came across a young bull elephant standing with one leg raised in the air. The elephant seemed distressed, so Mbembe approached it very carefully. He got down on one knee and inspected the elephant's foot and found a large piece of wood deeply embedded in it. As carefully and as gently as he could, Mbembe worked the wood out with his hunting knife,

---

[12] Larkin, 217.

after which the elephant gingerly put down its foot. The elephant turned to face the man, and with a rather curious look on its face, stared at him for several tense moments. Mbembe stood frozen, thinking of nothing else but being trampled. Eventually the elephant trumpeted loudly, turned and walked away. Twenty years later, Mbembe was walking through the Chicago Zoo. As he approached the elephant enclosure, one of the creatures turned and walked over to near where Mbembe was standing. The large bull elephant stared at Mbembe, lifted its front foot off the ground, and then put it down. The elephant did that several times then trumpeted loudly, all the while staring at the man. Remembering the encounter in 1986, Mbembe couldn't help wondering if this was the same elephant. Mbembe summoned up his courage, climbed over the railing and made his way into the enclosure. He walked right up to the elephant and stared back in wonder. The elephant trumpeted again, wrapped its trunk around one of Mbembe's legs and slammed him against the railing, killing him instantly. Probably wasn't the same elephant.

Mbembe should have differentiated between these two animals more carefully. Likewise, Christians must use their discernment to carefully differentiate between two types of social situations. They are "A-social" situations and "Anti-social" situations. A-social situations are a different animal from anti-social situations. The prior one will get you killed and the latter one won't. An anti-social situation is one wherein you can use your social skills, (negotiation, capitulation, silence, distraction, apology, non-threatening posture, flight) to defuse hostility and disengage from a confrontation. Examples of the "anti-social" type of situation would be an obnoxious neighbor who lets his dog poop in your yard when you've asked him not to, an overly aggressive driver who darts in and steals the parking spot you've been waiting for with your blinker on, or a drunken football fan who spills beer down the back of your shirt. You never want to escalate an antisocial situation with verbal abuse, physical posturing, or intimidation. It is unnecessary, dangerous and potentially violent. Once violence is introduced into the equation you cannot control the degree of said violence. You might think, "I'm going to teach this guy a lesson but I won't go any further than that" but you have no way of knowing or controlling how "far" it will in fact go. Every violent encounter is potentially maiming and/or life-threatening. You don't control him, his friends and family, his future retaliatory actions, the unintended severity of the injuries you inflict, etc. You don't want to go there. It is not worth it and it is not Christian. As far as it depends upon you don't ever let it get to that point. Be the peacemaker. As Paul writes in **Romans 12:18: "If possible, so far as it depends upon you, be at peace with all men."** This is the wisdom of "turn the other cheek." This is the prudence of "turn the other cheek." This is the brilliance of "turn the other cheek." And this is your opportunity to turn the other cheek. Your goal is to use your social skills to defuse, de-escalate and disengage.

An a-social situation, on the other hand, is forced upon you so that you have no choice but to defend yourself and/or your loved ones. Examples of a-social confrontations would include such things as a home invasion, a rape attempt, a car jacking, or an encounter with a face-eating zombie who's high on bath salts. These are situations you didn't ask for and never saw coming. These are situations in which you are suddenly blind-sided by violence and find yourself in a fight or die predicament.

A good way to tell the difference between an anti-social situation and an a-social situation is the existence or non-existence of options. If someone is yelling at you, or gesturing at you, or challenging you to the extent that you are asking yourself, "Should I respond to this with violence or can I get myself out of it in some other way?" then the situation is probably anti-social and the answer is almost invariably "No I shouldn't respond with violence." The fact that you even have an option for non-violent action is the giveaway. In an a-social situation you simply have no other choice.

Proverbs 19:11 "A man's wisdom gives him patience; it is to his glory to overlook an offense."
Here are ten reasons to practice restraint when insulted:
1) Jesus commanded restraint.
2) Jesus practiced restraint and calls us to his example.
3) Restraint leaves room for God's vengeance and justice while retaliation makes you the judge, jury and executioner.
4) Restraint defuses; retaliation escalates and complicates.
5) Restraint joins us to Christ in the fellowship of his suffering and leads to further sanctification. Retaliation retards spiritual growth.
6) Restraint is an act of faith; retaliation is an act of doubt.
7) Restraint is an act of love; retaliation is an act of hate.
8) Restraint is an act of humility; retaliation is an act of pride.
9) Restraint is the moral high ground; retaliation joins the offender in the gutter.
10) Restraint makes future evangelism possible; retaliation closes the door to the gospel.

PART FOUR

COUNTERING POTENTIAL OBJECTIONS

Pacifists might point out that there is no example in the New Testament of Christians exercising self-defense (which is arguable). But the reverse actually is true - there is no example in the New Testament of a Christian who actually chose to die at the hands of a criminal rather than defend himself. In addition, there is no explicit instruction in the New Testament letters regarding how to respond if attacked by a murderous criminal. Therefore, the legitimacy of Christian self-defense in that circumstance must be determined on the basis of reasoning from the Biblical principles involved. Now let us consider various anticipated objections to the use of force in self-defense in light of Biblical principles.

1. THE MARTYRDOM OBJECTION

Some might argue that the martyrdoms resulting from the religious persecution of the early Christians recorded in the New Testament suggests a Biblical precedent for passive non-resistance to violence even if it results in one's own death. Two examples of such martyrdom include Stephen (Acts 6-7) and James (Acts 12:1-2). However, these two examples of martyrdom are not, strictly speaking, situations where self-defense was an actual possibility. First, this was "official" persecution at the hands of government agents: the Jewish council in the case of Stephen, and King Herod in the case of James. In most cases where one is arrested, detained, confronted or persecuted by government agents one does not have the opportunity, and in some cases not even the legal right, to defend oneself. The Biblical right to self-defense in such circumstances becomes a moot point. This was certainly the case for these two men in that they had no opportunity to defend themselves.

Secondly, both of these men were faced with overwhelming force to such a degree that any physical resistance, even if possible, would have been futile. Stephen was not in a position to offer meaningful resistance to the Jewish council, the false witnesses and the other elements that comprised the angry mob that had assembled to do him violence. James, imprisoned by King Herod, was certainly in no position to offer meaningful resistance to the soldier(s) sent to behead him in his cell. Furthermore, although not all martyrdoms are alike, many if not most religious martyrdoms that have occurred historically share these types of circumstances that would seem to preclude self-defense because there was no realistic opportunity to do so. **"Most Christians in history have had only the choice of endurance in the face of suffering. Some can flee. Some can fight for justice, but most endure suffering."**[13]

Therefore, the fact that Christian martyrs are recorded in the pages of scripture and history is not necessarily a valid argument against the legitimacy of self-defense for

---

[13] Stoyan Zaimov, Christian Post interview with William Taylor, co-editor of "Sorrow and Blood: Christian Mission in Contexts of Suffering, Persecution, and Martyrdom", http:www.christianpost.com/news/sorrow-blood-resource-chronicles-centuries-of-christian-suffering-persecution-and-martyrdom-107839/pageall.html (Oct. 31, 2013).

Christians because death by martyrdom and death by criminal homicide are not analogous.

What martyrdom does illustrate is the degree to which these Christian victims have embraced Jesus' teaching that whoever loses his life for Christ's sake will find it. The gospel emphasizes the value of eternal life over our brief life on this earth. Over and over again the scriptures emphasize that we are not to cling too dearly to our lives on this side of the grave. Relatively speaking, even those among us who may live to be centenarians have been like a mist that appears briefly and is then gone. That being the case, if we are ever forced to choose between a few more days or years of life by denying Christ on the one hand, or faithfulness to Christ via a martyr's death on the other hand, the Bible is clear that we would be wise to choose faithfulness and death. As John records in **Revelation 12:11** "**they did not love their life even when faced with death.**"

2. THE CRUCIFIXION OBJECTION

Martyrdom is not co-equivalent to passive non-resistance to a criminal attack. The only possible exception would be the crucifixion of Jesus himself. But the total uniqueness of Jesus' voluntary substitutionary death on the cross means that it is not a truly analogous comparison to a Christian self-defense scenario. Consider the following reasons.

1) The point of Jesus' death was to satisfy the wrath of God on our behalf and provide the means whereby we could be forgiven and reconciled to God. As the sinless Son of God Jesus was uniquely qualified to take the punishment of death upon himself in the place of others thus extending the gracious offer of "penalty-paid-righteousness" in exchange for faith. As a sinful creature you are not qualified to die "for" someone else in this respect. In this way Jesus' death is not analogous to a self-defense scenario in which you might be involved.

2) The extent to which Jesus' death is an example for Christians is necessarily limited. Obviously not all Christians are called to literally die on crosses. The New Testament writers do not apply Jesus' death on the cross as an example to his followers in the sense that they are to practice passive non-resistance to murderers. They apply Jesus' death on the cross as an example for Christians in that we are to deny ourselves (Matthew 16:24), die to sin (Romans 6:11), and have an attitude of trust in God when faced with unjust suffering (I Peter 2:21).

Granted, as Christians we are called to follow in Jesus' steps by enduring unjust suffering when it is forced upon us and we have no choice, i.e. the servant unfairly abused by his master (I Peter 2:18). That is simply a case of controlling the one thing we actually do control in a circumstance of unequal, inescapable and abusive authority - our attitude. We see Paul teaching the same thing to slaves in his first letter to the Corinthian Church basically telling them that if they were slaves when they were converted to Christ not to worry about it since they can't change that circumstance, but to continue to maintain a good Christian attitude. However, he goes on to say that if they can gain their freedom, thereby changing those circumstances, then they should do so (I Corinthians 7:21). But Christians are nowhere called to endure a violent and potentially life-threatening attack when someone attempts to force it on them and they do have a choice. For example, in the city of Lystra, the Apostle Paul was stoned by a violent mob and left for dead (Acts 14:19). But in the city of Jerusalem when Paul was about to be unjustly and illegally scourged by a soldier he asserted his rights as a Roman citizen, successfully preventing this abuse from taking place (Acts 22:25). In the first attack Paul endured a potentially life-threatening beating. In the second attack Paul successfully prevented a potentially life-threatening beating. What was the difference between these two violent attacks? The only differences between these two attacks were the options available to Paul. Paul had no defensive options in the first attack and therefore no choice but to endure it. Paul had a clear defensive option in the second attack and therefore he had a genuine choice, which he was quick to exercise. When Paul had a choice to defend himself against violence he did so, seeing no conflict between the exercise of self-defense and the command to take up his cross to follow Jesus.

3. THE EVANGELISM OBJECTION

In online discussion forums on this subject I have encountered the argument that the use of lethal force in self-defense is incompatible with Christianity because it precludes any possibility of future evangelism to the antagonist thus dispatched by you. Therefore, by selfishly choosing to preserve your life at the expense of his life you are in effect choosing to end all of his opportunities for salvation and consigning his soul to the eternal fires of hell. The "Christian" thing to do is to let him kill you because, after all, you are already saved. If he lives he might repent at some point in the future and then, if that happens, the two of you can sing kumbaya together one day in Heaven. I call this evangelistic technique, "passive-victim-evangelism" (PVE).

Granted you do have the option to forfeit your life to an attacker based upon this rationale if you so choose. As stated earlier, it is your life and therefore your choice to defend it or to sacrifice it on behalf of someone else to the glory of God as you see fit.

Having said that, there are some mitigating factors that prevent this course of action from being logically or scripturally compulsory for a Christian.

First, the (presumably) unbelieving antagonist who is seeking to do you great bodily harm has placed himself in a position whereby his life could potentially be forfeited. This was his choice not your choice. Your choice to defend yourself might conclude his evangelistic opportunities, but only in a secondary sense, not in the primary sense. You are not responsible for another person's foolish, risky or illegal choices that result in his death and lost opportunities for salvation. When a person decides to attempt to murder someone else they have chosen to risk forfeiture of their own life in the execution of that crime whether that forfeiture comes at the hands of the intended victim via legal/moral/ethical self-defense, or at the hands of the police who arrive in time to stop him by using lethal force, or through the judicial system which apprehends him after the fact, convicts him of murder and sentences him to fry in "Old Sparkey." The intended Christian victim is no more obligated to substitute her life for a murderer in the first instance than she is in the second two.

Secondly, the same rationale could be used to suggest that a Christian is obligated to go to any given unbeliever who is about to die from heart disease for want of a heart transplant, or liver disease for want of a liver transplant, and give up his life in order to provide these vital organs to the unbeliever. In this way the unbeliever would continue living to possibly repent another day while you, who are already saved, could proceed directly to Heaven without passing "Go" or collecting $200. But no one seriously suggests that this is a Christian obligation to unbelievers. There is no stampede of pacifist Christians lining up at the local hospital demanding the opportunity to forfeit their vital organs for the unbelieving patients waiting to receive critical, life-extending transplants.

Thirdly, in the moral math used to calculate the evangelistic cost-benefit of sacrificing your life to a murderer, his lost opportunity for future salvation may be an "x-factor" but is not necessarily the deciding factor of the equation. Considering the unpredictable nature of the numerous potential consequences of "passive-victim-evangelism," it's quite possible that the net evangelistic effect of such a course of action would be fewer souls saved not more.

For instance, consider that the thug whom you passively allowed to murder you might go on to murder one or more others who themselves were unbelievers thus precluding future evangelistic opportunities for any and all of them. These are murders that would not have happened if you had put a stop to the criminal's murderous proclivities. Thus your passive non-resistance, far from achieving a greater good, actually contributed to the condemnation and eternal punishment of many others. This would be an evangelistic net loss.

Consider that some member of your surviving family might be so traumatized at the injustice of your violent and premature death that their faith is damaged or their receptivity to the gospel is diminished; another evangelistic net loss.

And what of the consequences to the Kingdom of your untimely murder? The Apostle Paul had a desire to go on living rather than die because he knew he had many more years of "fruitful labor" (Philippians 1:22) to offer in the service of the Lord. That's one reason Paul defended himself and was a proper steward of his life. What of your fruitful labor? What of the people that you might have evangelized and discipled? What of the leadership, influence, and resources you would have provided to your local church? What is the true cost to the Kingdom of your decision to passively allow someone to kill you? Is there any way for you to know?

The "passive-victim-evangelist" might answer these objections by saying "I will simply leave all of those unknowns to the providence of God." Then why not trust to the providence of God that you are supposed to defend yourself against this murderous gang-banger and as a result his future victims are saved and go to Heaven, the members of your own family are saved and go to Heaven, your future converts to Christ are all saved and go to Heaven, and the converts of the missionaries that you support financially are saved and go to Heaven?

"Passive-victim-evangelism" is no trump card over the Biblical right to self-defense.

4. THE GOVERNMENT OBJECTION

Some might object that it is the Biblical role of the state or the civil government to "protect and defend" it's citizens therefore Christian self-defense is unnecessary.

I find no reference in scripture to any kind of police force in ancient Israel whose purpose was to protect Israelite citizens from criminal attack. Paul writes in **Romans 13:4** that the civil authorities are **"God's servants, agents of wrath to bring punishment on the wrongdoer."** Is "punishment" the same thing as "protection" or "defense?" No it is not. If the civil authorities apprehend your murderer and punish him they will have fulfilled their God-ordained role of punishment and vengeance, but they will not have protected you. There is no God-given mandate to government to protect citizens from criminal attack. There is only a God-given mandate to government to punish criminals after the fact.

In all honesty, civil authorities cannot protect most of the people most of the time - it is a physical impossibility. Police officers simply cannot be everywhere a crime of violence is occurring. Most of the time, their job is to investigate, pursue criminals and make arrests after a crime has been committed.

This inconvenient truth is reflected in the current status of police law in the United States of America. *"A government and its agents are under no general duty to provide public services, such as police protection, to any particular individual citizen." "The duty to provide public service is owed to the public at large, and, absent a special relationship between the police and an individual, no specific legal duty exists."*[14] Those are the opinions

---

[14] James W. Porter II, "America's 1st Freedom," November 2013, page 10

of the District of Columbia Superior Court and the D.C. Court of Appeals issued in 1978 and 1981 blocking a suit by three young women who had been raped and beaten for 14 hours during a nightmarish home invasion in 1975. Two of the women had repeatedly called the D.C. police. They watched a police car slowly roll by their townhouse after their first call for help, then were told help was on its way in subsequent calls, when indeed it was not. The decisions in that case, Warren v. District of Columbia, came at a time when D.C. was still enforcing its ban on firearms in the home for self-defense. The decision by those lower courts in Warren mirrored decades of U.S. Supreme Court precedents. The latest high-court opinion declaring police have no duty to protect ordinary citizens was handed down in June 2005.[15]

The simple truth is, were individual citizens owed an absolute duty to individual protection by police, no law enforcement agency in the nation could exist because of the glut of litigation claiming violation of individuals' rights to police protection.

Of course there are cases wherein the local police do protect and prevent violent crime. The point here is that protection is not the Biblical charge to civil government nor is it the legal requirement in current American jurisprudence. The charge to civil government, from both godly and secular perspectives, regarding criminal activity, is not prevention before the fact; it is punishment after the fact.

5. THE PERSECUTION OBJECTION

Some might object that passive submission to violent persecution advances the gospel more so than does self-defense. There is a presumption among some Christians that the church actually thrives under persecution as in, "Kill a Christian and ten more will spring up to take his

---

[15] Porter, 10

place." The truth is that sometimes the Church thrives under persecution and sometimes it doesn't and sometimes it depends upon what you mean by "thrive." Wheaten College theology professor Marc Cortez writes:

The main reason the argument seems to work is that we're most familiar with those instances where the church appears to have thrived under persecution. And that makes sense. We like to tell those stories. Who wants to talk about when things went badly? That's no fun. So we forget about the church in North Africa that was once the thriving heartland of Christianity, but after the Muslim invasions, the church slowly receded into the background before fading entirely. And we fail to talk about Asia Minor (especially after the 14th century) and Japan (after Christianity was outlawed in the 17th century), other instances where persecution had disastrous consequences for the church. I often have my students read a letter that Pliny wrote to the Emperor Trajan in the second century. After describing a variety of oppressive measures used to persecute early Christians, Pliny describes what happened. "There is no shadow of doubt that the temples, which have been almost deserted, are beginning to be frequented once more, that the sacred rites which have been long neglected are being renewed, and that sacrificial victims are for sale everywhere, whereas, till recently, a buyer was rarely to be found. From this it is easy to imagine what a host of men could be set right, were they given a chance of recantation." As Pliny describes things, it sure doesn't sound like the church is thriving. Instead, persecution has limited the growth of the church, bringing people back to paganism. These examples don't prove that Christianity can't thrive under persecution any more than the other examples prove that it always does. The point is just to demonstrate that the historical realities aren't as simple as we often suggest.[16]

When discussing the rightness or wrongness of exercising lethal force in self-defense, one cannot

---

[16] Marc Cortez, "Does the Church Thrive Under Persecution," Christianity.com, http:www.christianity.com/church/does-the-church-thrive-under-persectuion.html, March 28, 2014.

necessarily conclude that it is always wrong on the grounds that passive submission to persecution advances the Kingdom. Can God use your passive non-resistance and resulting death for good? Yes, he certainly can. God can also use your judicious exercise of force in self-defense for good. So why not follow the advice of Moses when the choice between life and death presents itself and "choose life" (Deuteronomy 30:19).

CONCLUSION

Archimedes said, "Give me a place to stand and with a lever I will move the whole world."[17] Spiritually speaking, the gospel is the lever that moves the world. Physically speaking, our brief lives here on planet earth represent our "place to stand," our fulcrum for the lever of the gospel. The church is a spiritual kingdom. We wrestle against a spiritual enemy. Our weapons are spiritual weapons. But in order to fight our spiritual battle with our spiritual weapons against our spiritual enemy we must maintain a physical existence for as long as God grants us life. For you, your life is the ground upon which the gospel fulcrum rests. Stand your ground.

---

[17] http://www.en.wikiquote.org/wiki/Archimides

WORKS CITED

Allen, John L.   The Global War on Christians is the Unreported   Catastrophe   of   our   Times. <www.christianpost.com>. November 15, 2013

Acquinas, St. Thomas.   The Summa Theologica, Second and   Revised   Edition,   1920.   March   26,   2014. <http://www.newadvent.org/summa/3064.htm/>

Berrigan, Philip.   Fighting the Lamb's War: Skirmishes with the American Empire. iUniverse.com, 1996,

Caile, John. Concealed Carry Magazine. May/June 2013. Cortez,   Marc.   Does   the   Church   Thrive   Under Persecution?   Christianity.com,   28   March2014. <http://www.christianty.com>

Cottrell, Jack. JUST WAR? - A Valid Concept. Christian Standard, November 5,2006.

Holmes, Arthur F.   War and Christian Ethics.   Baker, 1975.

Larkin, Tim.   How to Survive the Most Critical Five Seconds of Your Life. Vervante, April 11, 2012

NEW AMERICAN STANDARD BIBLE®, Copyright ©1960,1962,1963,1968,1971,1972,1973,1975,1977,1995 by The Lockman Foundation.

Porter, James W. America's 1st Freedom. November 2013.

Schaff, Philip. Nicene and Post-Nicene Fathers, First Series, Vol. 1. Buffalo, NY: Christian Literature Publishing Co., 1887. March 26, 2014 <http://www.newadvent.org/fathers/1102047.htm>

THE HOLY BIBLE, NEW INTERNATIONAL VERSION®, NIV® Copyright © 1973,1978, 1984, 2011 by Biblica, Inc.®

Zaimov, Stoyan. Christian Post, <http:www.christianpost.com>. Oct. 31, 2013.

Made in the USA
Middletown, DE
05 November 2014